America Unmasked: Exploring The Top 20 Issues Shaping The United States

Copyright

Copyright © 2024 by DR.MARC REGAN

DR.MARC REGAN asserts the moral right to be identified as the author of this work.

Dedication

I dedicate this book to my family, whose love and support have been my constant source of strength and inspiration. Without their unwavering presence in my life, I would not have been able to pursue my passion for writing and bring this book to fruition.

Table of Contents

20. Trade Policies: Navigating Global Partnerships

Introduction

America Unmasked: Exploring The Top 20 Issues Shaping The United States is a comprehensive guide that delves into the most pressing concerns facing the United States today. Authored by a group of esteemed political analysts, this book offers an in-depth exploration of the key issues that are shaping the social, political, and economic landscape of the nation.

One of the fundamental aspects of this book is its ability to provide an unbiased and objective analysis of the topics at hand. Each issue is thoroughly researched and presented from multiple perspectives, allowing readers to gain a comprehensive understanding of the complexities surrounding each topic.

From the economy to healthcare, from immigration to climate change, America Unmasked covers a wide range of issues that have significant implications for the nation. The authors have carefully curated the list of topics, ensuring that they represent the most critical and pertinent issues facing the United States in the 21st century.

The book is not just a compilation of facts and figures, but also offers insight into the historical context and the potential future implications of these issues. In doing so, it fosters critical thinking and informed discourse, encouraging readers to engage with the material and form their own opinions.

Moreover, the book is written in a clear and accessible language, making it suitable for a wide range of audiences. Whether you are a student, a policy-maker, or simply a concerned citizen, America Unmasked offers a valuable resource for anyone seeking to understand the complex challenges facing the United States.

Furthermore, the book serves as a call to action, urging readers to actively engage with the issues and become part of the solution. By shedding light on these crucial topics, the authors hope to inspire meaningful conversations and spark positive change in the country.

In conclusion, America Unmasked: Exploring The Top 20 Issues Shaping The United States is a thought-provoking and timely exploration of the most significant challenges facing the nation. Through its comprehensive analysis and engaging narrative, the book provides a valuable resource for anyone seeking to deepen their understanding of the United States' most pressing concerns.

1. Income Inequality: Bridging the Wealth Gap

Income inequality refers to the unequal distribution of income within a population. It has been a persistent issue in the United States, with the wealthiest individuals holding a disproportionate amount of the nation's wealth while a large percentage of the population struggles to make ends meet. This wealth gap has far-reaching consequences for the economy and society as a whole, and addressing income inequality is crucial for creating a more equitable and just society.

The United States has one of the highest levels of income inequality among developed countries. According to the Pew Research Center, the top 20% of American households earned more than 50% of the total income in 2018, while the bottom 20% earned just 3%. This unequal distribution of income has only worsened in recent decades, with the top 1% of earners seeing their incomes grow at a much faster rate than the rest of the population.

One of the main drivers of income inequality in the United States is the growing disparity in wages. While the incomes of top earners have soared, wages for the average American worker have stagnated. This trend is further exacerbated by the decline of labor unions and the outsourcing of jobs to countries with lower labor costs. As a result, many working-class individuals are struggling to make a living and provide for their families, while a small percentage of the population enjoys unprecedented wealth.

Income inequality has far-reaching consequences for the economy and society as a whole. It hinders economic growth by limiting the purchasing power of the majority of the population, who are unable to afford goods and services that drive economic activity. This, in turn, leads to decreased demand for products and services, which can ultimately lead to job losses and a slowdown in economic growth. Additionally, income inequality contributes to social unrest and can lead to increased crime rates and political instability.

Bridging the wealth gap in the United States will require a multi-faceted approach. One of the most effective measures is to raise the minimum wage to a level that provides a living wage for all workers. This will ensure that even the lowest-paid workers are able to afford the basic necessities of life and contribute to the economy. Additionally, implementing progressive tax policies that require the wealthiest individuals and corporations to pay their fair share will help address income inequality.

Income inequality has long been a significant issue in society, with the gap between the rich and the poor continuing to widen. Bridging this wealth gap has become a priority for governments, organizations, and individuals alike, as it is crucial for the well-being and stability of our communities. In this essay, I will explore the causes and consequences of income inequality, as well as the potential solutions to bridge this gap.

The causes of income inequality are complex and multifaceted. Factors such as globalization, technological advancements, and changes in the labor market have all contributed to the widening gap between the rich and the poor. Globalization has led to increased competition and outsourcing, which has resulted in job losses and wage stagnation for many workers. Technological advancements have also played a role, as automation and artificial intelligence have replaced many low-skilled jobs, further exacerbating income inequality.

Consequences of income inequality are far-reaching and detrimental to society as a whole. Inequality has been linked to higher rates of poverty, crime, and social unrest. It also has negative implications for health, education, and overall quality of life. Additionally, income inequality can lead to a lack of social mobility, as those born into poverty often struggle to escape it, perpetuating the cycle of poverty for generations.

Bridging the wealth gap requires a multi-faceted approach, and there is no one-size-fits-all solution. However, there are several measures that can be taken to address income inequality. One potential solution is to implement progressive tax policies that require the wealthy to pay a higher percentage of their income in taxes. This would help redistribute wealth and provide funding for social welfare programs aimed at reducing poverty and inequality.

Additionally, increasing the minimum wage and ensuring that all workers have access to quality healthcare and education are crucial steps in addressing income inequality. Investing in education and job training programs can also help provide individuals with the skills they need to secure higher-paying jobs and improve their economic prospects.

Furthermore, promoting inclusive economic growth and addressing structural barriers to opportunity is essential in bridging the wealth gap. This includes addressing systemic racism and discrimination, as well as promoting diversity and inclusion in the workplace. Additionally, providing support for small businesses and entrepreneurs in marginalized communities can help create opportunities for economic advancement.

In conclusion, income inequality is a pressing issue that must be addressed in order to create a more equitable and just society. It is imperative that governments, organizations, and individuals work together to implement policies and programs aimed at reducing poverty and bridging the wealth gap. By taking a comprehensive and multi-faceted approach to addressing income inequality, we can build a more prosperous and inclusive society for all.

2. Healthcare Crisis: Navigating Access and Affordability

The healthcare crisis in America is a complex issue that has been a topic of concern for many years. Access to healthcare and its affordability are two significant challenges that impact the American population. As the debate on healthcare reform continues, it is important to understand the implications of these challenges and explore potential solutions.

The issue of access to healthcare is multifaceted. Many Americans face barriers to accessing healthcare services due to factors such as lack of health insurance, limited healthcare facilities in rural areas, and long wait times for appointments. These issues are particularly prevalent in underserved communities, where residents may not have the means to travel to larger cities for medical care. Additionally, the rising cost of healthcare has made it increasingly difficult for individuals to afford necessary treatments and medications.

The Affordable Care Act (ACA) was a significant step in addressing the issue of access to healthcare by expanding Medicaid and creating health insurance marketplaces. However, the Trump administration's efforts to dismantle the ACA and the recent Supreme Court ruling on the individual mandate have raised concerns about the future of healthcare access in America. It is crucial for policymakers to prioritize expanding access to healthcare for all Americans, regardless of their income or employment status.

Affordability is another major concern in the realm of healthcare. The cost of healthcare services and prescription medications has been steadily rising, making it difficult for many individuals to afford the care they need. This has resulted in a significant number of Americans forgoing necessary medical treatments or medications due to financial constraints. The burden of medical debt has also had a devastating impact on many families, leading to financial instability and hardship.

Addressing the affordability of healthcare requires comprehensive reform that tackles the root causes of rising costs. This includes addressing the high prices of prescription medications, reducing administrative costs, and implementing measures to control healthcare spending. Additionally, promoting preventative care and investing in public health initiatives can help reduce the need for costly medical interventions in the long run.

In navigating the healthcare crisis in America, it is essential for policymakers to prioritize the needs of the American people. This includes ensuring that every individual has access to affordable healthcare services and that no one is left behind due to financial constraints. It is also critical to address the underlying factors contributing to the rising costs of healthcare, and to work towards creating a more equitable and sustainable healthcare system for all.

The healthcare crisis in America is a pressing issue that requires immediate attention and action. With challenges of access and affordability looming over the population, it is imperative to address these issues head-on in order to create a healthcare system that is inclusive, affordable, and accessible for all Americans.

Access to healthcare is a fundamental right, yet many individuals in the United States struggle to obtain the care they need. Whether it is due to financial constraints, lack of health insurance, or limited availability of healthcare providers, the barriers to access are evident. This has resulted in a disproportionate impact on marginalized and vulnerable populations, further exacerbating health disparities.

The cost of healthcare is also a significant concern for many Americans. The rising expenses of medical services, prescription drugs, and insurance premiums are placing a heavy burden on individuals and families. As a result, many are forced to make difficult choices between their health and financial stability, which should never be the case in a developed and prosperous nation.

In order to address the healthcare crisis, collaboration and cooperation between policymakers, healthcare providers, and the public are essential. This would require a multi-faceted approach that addresses the root causes of the crisis and implements long-term solutions. For instance, policies that expand access to affordable health insurance, increase funding for community health centers, and incentivize healthcare providers to serve underserved areas can help to alleviate the barriers to access. Additionally, measures to lower the cost of prescription drugs and medical services, as well as initiatives to promote preventive care and wellness, can contribute to making healthcare more affordable for all.

Moreover, there needs to be a concerted effort to prioritize the well-being of the American population. This involves recognizing healthcare as a fundamental human right and ensuring that everyone has access to high-quality, comprehensive care. It also requires a shift in the cultural and societal perception of healthcare, where preventive care, mental health services, and holistic approaches to wellness are valued and supported.

In conclusion, the healthcare crisis in America is a complex and multifaceted issue that requires immediate attention and action. By addressing the challenges of access and affordability, we can work towards creating a healthcare system that is inclusive, affordable, and accessible for all Americans. This will necessitate collaboration and cooperation between policymakers, healthcare providers, and the public to address the root causes of the crisis and implement long-term solutions. By prioritizing the well-being of the American population, we

can create a healthcare system that truly serves
the needs of all.

3. Climate Change: The Urgent Battle for a Sustainable Future

Climate change has become one of the most pressing issues of our time, with the urgent need for action becoming more and more apparent. In America, the battle for a sustainable future is becoming increasingly critical as the impacts of climate change continue to be felt across the country. From extreme weather events to rising sea levels and melting ice caps, the evidence of climate change is undeniable. The time for action is now, and the stakes could not be higher.

One of the key challenges facing America in the fight against climate change is the need to transition towards a more sustainable and environmentally friendly energy system. The reliance on fossil fuels has been a major contributor to the greenhouse gas emissions that are driving climate change. It is clear that a shift towards renewable energy sources such as solar, wind, and hydro power is essential in order to reduce emissions and mitigate the impacts of climate change.

The urgency of this transition is underscored by the increasingly severe weather events that are becoming more common across the country. From devastating hurricanes in the Gulf Coast to record-breaking wildfires in the West, the impacts of climate change are being felt in every corner of America. The need for resilient infrastructure and disaster preparedness is becoming increasingly clear, as communities are being forced to adapt to the new normal of a changing climate.

In addition to the environmental impacts, the economic and social costs of climate change are also becoming more evident. The disruptions to agriculture, infrastructure, and public health that are being caused by climate change carry significant costs that will only continue to grow if action is not taken. It is clear that the battle for a sustainable future is not only an environmental imperative, but also an economic and social necessity.

Fortunately, there are many opportunities for positive action in the fight against climate change. From investing in clean energy infrastructure to implementing policies that encourage sustainable practices, there are many avenues for progress. It is clear that the transition towards a sustainable future will require collaboration and cooperation across all levels of government, as well as the private sector and civil society.

The challenges ahead in the battle for a sustainable future are significant, but the urgency of the situation demands bold and decisive action. This issue is not just an environmental concern, but a moral imperative for the well-being of current and future generations. It is crucial that America takes the lead in this fight and sets an example for the rest of the world to follow.

The impacts of climate change are being felt across the United States, from extreme weather events to rising sea levels and diminishing natural resources. These effects are a call to action, signaling the need for immediate and comprehensive measures to mitigate and adapt to the changing climate. Transitioning towards a more sustainable energy system, building resilient infrastructure, and implementing policies that encourage sustainability are all crucial steps in this battle.

The urgency of the situation cannot be overstated. The ramifications of inaction are dire and will reverberate for generations to come. The moral imperative to act in the face of these challenges is clear. We have a responsibility to safeguard the environment and the well-being of all living beings. This responsibility extends not only to our own generation but to those that will come after us.

It is essential that America takes the lead in this fight for a sustainable future. As one of the world's largest economies and emitters of greenhouse gases, the actions and policies of the United States have a significant impact on the global effort to combat climate change. By taking bold and decisive actions, America can inspire and influence other nations to follow suit.

The battle for a sustainable future is a complex and multifaceted endeavor that requires collaborative efforts from government, businesses, and individuals. It necessitates long-term planning, investment, and collective action. But the time for action is now. The future of our planet and our society depends on the choices and actions we make today.

In conclusion, the urgent battle for a sustainable future in America is one of the most pressing issues of our time. The importance of this fight cannot be overstated. It is not just a matter of environmental conservation; it is a moral imperative for the well-being of current and future generations. Transitioning towards sustainability and combating climate change are essential for the future of our planet, and it is imperative that America takes the lead in this endeavor. The time for action is now.

4. Gun Control: Balancing Rights and Public Safety

Gun control has been a highly debated topic in America for many years. On one hand, there are those who believe in the right to bear arms as outlined in the Second Amendment of the U.S. Constitution. On the other hand, there are those who are concerned about the public safety implications of widespread gun ownership. The challenge lies in finding a balance between these two conflicting perspectives.

The Second Amendment of the U.S. Constitution states that "A well regulated Militia, being necessary to the security of a free State, the right of the people to keep and bear Arms, shall not be infringed." This has been interpreted by many as the right for individuals to own and carry firearms for personal protection and self-defense. However, in light of the increasing prevalence of mass shootings and gun violence in America, there has been growing concern about the need for stricter gun control measures to ensure public safety.

One of the main arguments in favor of gun control is the need to prevent gun violence. According to the Centers for Disease Control and Prevention, there were over 39,000 firearm-related deaths in the United States in 2019. This included homicides, suicides, and unintentional shootings. The availability of firearms has been linked to higher rates of gun violence, and many believe that implementing stricter gun control measures, such as universal background checks and bans on assault weapons, could help reduce these alarming statistics.

On the other hand, proponents of gun rights argue that restricting access to firearms infringes upon their constitutional rights and hinders their ability to defend themselves and their families. They also point to the fact that many gun owners are law-abiding citizens who should not be penalized for the actions of a few individuals. They argue that the focus should be on addressing the root causes of gun violence, such as mental health issues and societal factors, rather than simply implementing stricter gun control measures.

Finding a balance between these two perspectives is a complex and challenging task. It requires careful consideration of individual rights and public safety, and it may involve compromises from both sides. For example, while it is important to protect the right to bear arms, it is also crucial to implement policies that prevent guns from falling into the wrong hands. This could involve comprehensive background checks, mental health screenings, and restrictions on certain types of firearms.

The issue of gun control in America is a complex and contentious one, with deeply held beliefs on both sides of the debate. On one hand, there is a strong emphasis on protecting individual rights, including the right to bear arms as outlined in the Second Amendment of the

United States Constitution. On the other hand, there is a pressing need to consider the safety and well-being of the public, as evidenced by the ongoing gun violence epidemic in the country. Finding a balance between these two perspectives is essential in developing effective gun control measures that address the concerns of both gun rights advocates and proponents of public safety.

It is imperative to recognize and respect the rights of individuals to own firearms for personal protection, hunting, and other lawful purposes. The Second Amendment has long been a cornerstone of American legal and cultural tradition, and any proposed gun control measures must take this into account. Restricting lawful gun ownership without justification would be a violation of the constitutional rights of American citizens.

At the same time, the prevalence of gun violence in the United States cannot be ignored. Mass shootings, homicides, and suicides involving firearms continue to be a significant public health issue, causing immense harm to individuals, families, and communities. In light of these sobering statistics, it is clear that some form of gun control is necessary to help reduce the risk of gun-related tragedies and promote public safety.

In addressing the issue of gun control, policymakers must engage in thoughtful and constructive dialogue to consider the diverse perspectives and find common ground. By fostering an environment of open communication and collaboration, it may be possible to identify areas of consensus and develop practical solutions that balance the rights of gun owners with the need to prevent gun violence. This approach requires a willingness to listen to opposing viewpoints and work towards finding a compromise that works for all Americans.

Effective gun control measures should prioritize responsible gun ownership while also implementing safeguards to prevent firearms from falling into the wrong hands. This could involve enacting universal background checks, implementing waiting periods for purchasing firearms, and improving mental health screening processes. Additionally, addressing the issue of illegal gun trafficking and improving access to mental health resources are crucial components of any comprehensive gun control strategy.

In conclusion, the issue of gun control in America demands a thoughtful and nuanced approach that respects the rights of individuals while prioritizing public safety. By finding common ground and working towards a balanced solution, policymakers can develop effective gun control measures that benefit all Americans. It is essential to engage in respectful and constructive dialogue to address this important issue and find a solution that works for the diverse range of stakeholders impacted by gun control policies. Ultimately, the goal should be to create a safer and more secure society while upholding the fundamental rights and liberties of the American people.

5. Immigration: Building Bridges, Overcoming Barriers

Immigration has always been a contentious issue in America, with debates often centering on the perceived benefits or detriments of welcoming foreign individuals into the country. While some argue that immigrants bring diversity, talent, and economic growth to the nation, others contend that their presence leads to job competition, strain on social services, and cultural clashes. Yet, amidst these conflicting perspectives, it is crucial to recognize that immigration is not just about building physical bridges but also about overcoming barriers, both real and imagined.

In the past, America has benefited immensely from the contributions of immigrants. The infusion of diverse cultural and intellectual perspectives has led to innovation and progress in various fields. From the construction of the transcontinental railroad by Chinese immigrants to the scientific breakthroughs made by foreign-born researchers, the impact of immigrants on American society is undeniable. Moreover, many immigrants arrive in pursuit of the American dream, willing to work hard and make sacrifices for a better future. Their ambition and resilience have strengthened the nation's workforce and bolstered its economy.

However, immigration also presents challenges that cannot be ignored. There are concerns about the strain placed on public services, such as healthcare and education, as well as the potential for cultural tensions to arise. Additionally, the issue of illegal immigration has sparked debates about national security and the rule of law. Valid as these concerns may be, they should not overshadow the fact that immigration has the potential to enhance the nation's social fabric and global standing.

To build bridges and overcome barriers, a comprehensive approach to immigration is needed. This involves recognizing the value of diversity and actively promoting the integration of immigrants into American society. It also requires addressing the root causes of migration, such as poverty, violence, and political instability, both domestically and globally. By facilitating legal pathways for immigrants to enter the country and fostering a more inclusive environment, America can harness the full potential of its immigrant population.

America has long been known as a melting pot, a nation built on the contributions of immigrants from all over the world. However, in recent years, the issue of immigration has become increasingly contentious, with debates raging over topics such as border security, asylum seekers, and refugee resettlement. While it is important to address the concerns and challenges associated with immigration, it is equally crucial to recognize and celebrate its many benefits.

At the same time, it is essential to acknowledge the significance of a secure and well-regulated immigration system. This entails enforcing immigration laws while also ensuring that they are fair and humane. A balanced approach that combines border security with compassionate policies for asylum seekers and refugees is necessary to maintain both the integrity of the nation's borders and its commitment to human rights.

The contributions of immigrants to American society cannot be understated. They bring diverse perspectives, skills, and talents that enrich the country and drive progress and innovation. Immigrants also play a vital role in the economy, filling critical labor shortages and starting businesses that create jobs and contribute to economic growth. Moreover, immigrants often take on jobs that are essential to the functioning of society, from healthcare and agriculture to construction and hospitality.

In addition to their economic contributions, immigrants also add cultural vibrancy to American communities. They bring with them traditions, cuisines, and customs that enrich the nation's social fabric. By embracing the diversity that immigrants bring, America can foster greater understanding and inclusion, creating a more vibrant and dynamic society.

It is crucial to recognize that the issue of immigration also presents challenges. It is important to address concerns about national security, the strain on public resources, and the impact of immigration on the labor market. However, these challenges must be met with thoughtful, evidence-based policies that aim to strike a balance between the needs of the country and the rights of immigrants.

At the same time, it is essential to acknowledge the significance of a secure and well-regulated immigration system. This entails enforcing immigration laws while also ensuring that they are fair and humane. A balanced approach that combines border security with compassionate policies for asylum seekers and refugees is necessary to maintain both the integrity of the nation's borders and its commitment to human rights.

In conclusion, immigration in America is a complex and multifaceted issue. To truly build bridges and overcome barriers, it is imperative for the country to approach the issue with compassion, pragmatism, and a long-term vision. By recognizing the contributions of immigrants and addressing the challenges they present, America can continue to thrive as a diverse and inclusive society. Through thoughtful and deliberate action, the nation can harness the strengths of immigration while minimizing its potential drawbacks, ultimately forging a brighter future for all.

6. Racial Inequality: Striving for a More Equitable Society

Racial inequality has been a persistent issue in America, one that has plagued the country since its inception. Despite significant progress in civil rights and social justice, racial disparities continue to exist in various areas of American society. From education to employment and the criminal justice system, people of color continue to face discrimination and disadvantages that hinder their opportunities for success. It is clear that addressing these disparities is crucial for building a more equitable society.

In the realm of education, racial inequality is evident in the disparities in resources and opportunities available to students of color. Minority students are more likely to attend underfunded schools with fewer resources, leading to lower academic achievement and graduation rates. Additionally, racial bias and discrimination can negatively impact the educational experiences of students of color, leading to disparities in discipline and access to advanced coursework. Addressing these disparities requires a comprehensive approach that includes increasing funding for schools in underserved communities, implementing anti-bias training for educators, and promoting diversity in curriculum and leadership.

In the workforce, people of color continue to face challenges related to employment opportunities and advancement. Studies have shown that racial minorities are more likely to experience discrimination in hiring and promotions, leading to higher rates of unemployment and underemployment. Additionally, the racial wage gap persists, with people of color earning less than their white counterparts for the same work. Addressing these disparities requires not only enforcing anti-discrimination laws but also implementing initiatives to promote diversity and inclusion in hiring and advancement practices.

Perhaps one of the most pressing issues related to racial inequality in America is the criminal justice system. People of color are disproportionately impacted by mass incarceration, police brutality, and disparate sentencing practices. The war on drugs, for example, has led to the disproportionate incarceration of black and brown individuals, perpetuating cycles of poverty and systemic disenfranchisement. Addressing these disparities requires a comprehensive approach that includes reforming sentencing practices, demilitarizing and diversifying law enforcement, and investing in rehabilitation and reentry programs for formerly incarcerated individuals.

In order to strive for a more equitable society, it is essential to address the disparities that exist on both a systemic and individual level. This means implementing policies and initiatives that promote equity and inclusion, as well as challenging and dismantling the systemic racism and bias that perpetuate these disparities. Furthermore, it requires ongoing education and advocacy to raise awareness and mobilize action to address racial inequality in all its forms.

At the systemic level, it is crucial to implement policies and initiatives that promote equity and inclusion. This can include measures such as affirmative action, diversity and inclusion training, and targeted support for marginalized communities. By actively working to level the playing field and provide opportunities for all, we can begin to address the systemic barriers that contribute to racial inequality.

Simultaneously, it is important to challenge and dismantle the systemic racism and bias that perpetuate these disparities. This involves examining the ways in which existing systems and institutions perpetuate racial inequality, and actively working to change them. This can include reforming criminal justice practices, addressing housing and employment discrimination, and advocating for more equitable representation in government and leadership positions. By actively working to dismantle the systems that perpetuate racial inequality, we can begin to create a more just and equitable society.

Beyond systemic change, it is also crucial to address racial inequality on an individual level. This requires ongoing education and advocacy to raise awareness and mobilize action to address racial inequality in all its forms. This can involve community outreach and engagement, cultural competency training, and efforts to promote empathy and understanding across racial lines. By actively working to change individual attitudes and behaviors, we can begin to create a society where everyone is treated with dignity and respect, regardless of their race or ethnicity.

In conclusion, striving for a more equitable society requires addressing racial disparities on both a systemic and individual level. This means implementing policies and initiatives that promote equity and inclusion, as well as challenging and dismantling the systemic racism and bias that perpetuate these disparities. It also requires ongoing education and advocacy to raise awareness and mobilize action to address racial inequality in all its forms. It is only through acknowledging and actively working to dismantle racial disparities that we can truly achieve justice and equality for all.

7. Education Reimagined: Unlocking Potential for All

Education is often seen as the key to unlocking potential and opportunity in America. However, the traditional model of education has faced criticisms for its inability to meet the needs and potential of all students. In recent years, there has been a growing movement to reimagine education in America in order to unlock the potential for all students.

One of the key elements of this movement is the recognition that the traditional one-size-fits-all model of education does not work for every student. Each student has their own unique needs, interests, and strengths, and the education system should be structured in a way that allows for individualized learning. This means moving away from a system that places heavy emphasis on standardized testing and instead focusing on personalized learning plans that cater to each student's abilities and interests.

In addition to individualized learning, education reimagined also emphasizes the importance of holistic development. This means going beyond just academic achievement and also focusing on the social, emotional, and physical well-being of students. The education system should provide opportunities for students to develop important life skills such as critical thinking, problem-solving, and communication, as well as promoting physical health and emotional intelligence.

Furthermore, the movement to reimagine education in America also emphasizes the importance of real-world learning experiences. This means providing students with opportunities to engage in hands-on, experiential learning that connects their education to the real world. This could include internships, apprenticeships, project-based learning, and community service, all of which provide students with the opportunity to apply their learning in practical settings.

Another important aspect of education reimagined is the recognition of the role of technology in education. Technology has the potential to greatly enhance the learning experience by providing access to a wide range of resources and opportunities for collaboration and creativity. This means integrating technology into the classroom in a way that enhances learning and allows students to develop critical digital literacy skills.

In order to truly unlock the potential for all students, the education system in America must also address equity and access. It is essential that all students, regardless of their background or circumstances, have access to high-quality education. This entails working to ensure that every student has the opportunity to reach their full potential, regardless of their socioeconomic status, race, or other factors that have historically limited access to quality education.

One of the key issues that the education system in America must address in order to promote equity and access is the disparity in school funding. It is no secret that schools in low-income areas often receive less funding than schools in more affluent areas, leading to significant differences in the quality of education offered. This perpetuates inequality and limits the opportunities of students from lower-income families. To truly unlock the potential of all students, funding must be allocated in a way that provides equal opportunities for all students, regardless of their zip code.

Reducing barriers to access for marginalized groups is another crucial aspect of promoting equity and access in education. This may involve implementing policies and programs that address the specific needs of students from marginalized communities, including students of color, students with disabilities, and English language learners. By providing additional support and resources to these students, the education system can ensure that they have equal access to high-quality education and the opportunity to succeed.

Additionally, providing support for students who may face additional challenges is essential for promoting equity and access in education. This could include programs and services aimed at addressing the social and emotional needs of students, as well as providing additional academic support for students who may be falling behind. By addressing the specific challenges that students face, the education system can create an environment where all students have the opportunity to thrive.

In conclusion, in order to truly unlock the potential of all students, the education system in America must prioritize equity and access. This requires addressing issues such as school funding disparities, reducing barriers to access for marginalized groups, and providing support for students who may face additional challenges. By prioritizing these efforts, the education system can create an environment where all students have the opportunity to receive a high-quality education and reach their full potential. Ultimately, by embracing these principles, the education system in America can truly unlock the potential of all students and prepare them for success in the future.

8. Political Polarization: Finding Common Ground in Divided Times

In today's political landscape, it feels as though there are two distinct and opposing ideologies that are constantly at odds with one another. This divisiveness has led to a growing sense of political polarization, making it increasingly difficult to find common ground in the midst of such divisiveness. However, in order to move forward and address the pressing issues facing our society, it is crucial that we find a way to bridge the gap between these differing viewpoints and work towards a more unified future.

One of the major factors contributing to political polarization is the rise of social media and 24-hour news cycles. These platforms have allowed individuals to curate their news and information sources, creating echo chambers where only their viewpoints are reinforced and validated. This has led to a reinforcement of pre-existing beliefs, making individuals less likely to engage with opposing viewpoints and more susceptible to extreme or radical ideologies. As a result, this has contributed to an "us vs. them" mentality, further deepening the divide between differing political ideologies.

Another contributing factor to political polarization is the emergence of identity politics. In today's society, individuals often align themselves with a particular political ideology based on aspects of their identity such as race, gender, or sexual orientation. This has led to a focus on group identity rather than a focus on common values and beliefs, further exacerbating the divide between differing political groups.

While it may seem daunting to find common ground in such a polarized political landscape, it is not impossible. One way to begin bridging the gap is by fostering constructive dialogue between individuals with differing viewpoints. This means actively listening to and considering the perspectives of others, even if they may not align with our own beliefs. By engaging in respectful and open-minded conversations, we can begin to break down the barriers that divide us and find common ground on which to build a more unified future.

In today's political landscape, it feels as though there are two distinct and opposing ideologies that are constantly at odds with one another. This divisiveness has led to a growing sense of political polarization, making it increasingly difficult to find common ground in the midst of such divisiveness. However, in order to move forward and address the pressing issues facing our society, it is crucial that we find a way to bridge the gap between these differing viewpoints and work towards a more unified future.

One of the major factors contributing to political polarization is the rise of social media and 24-hour news cycles. These platforms have allowed individuals to curate their news and information sources, creating echo chambers where only their viewpoints are reinforced and validated. This has led to a reinforcement of pre-existing beliefs, making individuals less likely to engage with opposing viewpoints and more susceptible to extreme or radical ideologies. As a result, this has contributed to an "us vs. them" mentality, further deepening the divide between differing political ideologies.

Another contributing factor to political polarization is the emergence of identity politics. In today's society, individuals often align themselves with a particular political ideology based on aspects of their identity such as race, gender, or sexual orientation. This has led to a focus on group identity rather than a focus on common values and beliefs, further exacerbating the divide between differing political groups.

While it may seem daunting to find common ground in such a polarized political landscape, it is not impossible. One way to begin bridging the gap is by fostering constructive dialogue between individuals with differing viewpoints. This means actively listening to and considering the perspectives of others, even if they may not align with our own beliefs. By engaging in respectful and open-minded conversations, we can begin to break down the barriers that divide us and find common ground on which to build a more unified future.

Additionally, it is crucial to focus on the values and beliefs that unite us rather than the issues that divide us. While there may be significant differences in policy opinions, there are often shared values that can serve as a foundation for finding common ground. By focusing on these shared values, such as a commitment to equality, justice, and compassion, we can begin to build a more collaborative and inclusive political landscape.

Ultimately, finding common ground in a politically polarized society requires a concerted effort from all individuals. It means being willing to engage with differing viewpoints, fostering constructive dialogue, and focusing on shared values. While the path towards unity may be challenging, it is essential in order to address the pressing issues facing our society and move towards a more inclusive and cohesive future. By recognizing the humanity in one another and working towards common goals, we can begin to break down the barriers of political polarization and build a more united society.

9. Infrastructure Revival: Rebuilding America's Backbone

Infrastructure is the backbone of any country's economy and society. It is the physical framework that supports the activities of businesses, communities, and individuals. From roads and bridges to water and sewage systems, the infrastructure plays a crucial role in maintaining the functioning of a nation. However, in recent years, the infrastructure in the United States has been in dire need of revival and rebuilding.

The state of the nation's infrastructure has been a topic of concern for many years. The American Society of Civil Engineers (ASCE) has regularly assessed the state of the country's infrastructure and has consistently given it poor grades. According to the ASCE's 2021 Report Card for America's Infrastructure, the overall grade was a

C- with many categories such as roads, bridges, and public transit receiving even lower grades. This is a stark reminder of the pressing need to invest in the revival of the nation's infrastructure.

The need for infrastructure revival in the United States is evident from the crumbling roads, structurally deficient bridges, and outdated water and sewage systems. Many of the country's roads are riddled with potholes and are in desperate need of repair. In addition, one out of every three bridges is in need of repair or replacement, posing a serious safety risk to the public. The water and sewage systems are also aging and in need of modernization to ensure the safety and health of the population.

The revival of America's infrastructure will require significant investment and a long-term commitment. The Biden administration has proposed a $2 trillion infrastructure plan, known as the American Jobs Plan, to address the nation's infrastructure needs. This plan aims to modernize the nation's infrastructure, create millions of jobs, and stimulate economic growth. The plan includes investments in transportation, water and energy systems, broadband access, and affordable housing, among other areas.

The revival of America's infrastructure will not only improve the safety and efficiency of the country's transportation and utilities but also create jobs and stimulate economic growth. Investing in infrastructure will create employment opportunities for construction workers, engineers, and other professionals. It will also support businesses and industries that rely on the infrastructure for their operations, such as transportation, logistics, and manufacturing.

Investing in infrastructure is a crucial aspect of maintaining and enhancing the quality of life for Americans. While the immediate benefits of job creation and economic growth are important, the long-term impact of modern and efficient infrastructure is equally significant. Modern transportation systems are essential in reducing traffic congestion, not only making travel more efficient but also improving air quality. Upgraded water and sewage systems ensure that all communities have access to clean and safe drinking water, a fundamental necessity for a high quality of life. Expanded broadband access connects more people to educational and economic opportunities, broadening the horizons and potentials of individuals and communities.

The state of America's infrastructure has reached a critical point, with crumbling roads, bridges, and outdated water and transportation systems. The current infrastructure is becoming increasingly inadequate to support the needs of a growing population, and it is crucial to address these issues to ensure the well-being and prosperity of all Americans.

Moreover, revitalizing the infrastructure also presents a bold opportunity to create millions of jobs, stimulate economic growth, and enhance the overall living standards for the American people. Construction projects, technology upgrades, and maintenance work will require a skilled workforce, creating employment opportunities across various sectors of the economy. These jobs can provide stability for individuals and families, boosting the economic well-being of communities.

Furthermore, investing in infrastructure will also have a positive impact on the overall economic growth of the nation. Improved transportation systems will facilitate the movement of goods and people, increasing productivity and efficiency. This, in turn, will drive economic growth and contribute to the nation's competitiveness on the global stage.

Clean and safe drinking water is a basic necessity, and it is imperative that all communities have access to it. Upgraded water and sewage systems are essential not only for health and well-being but also for attracting investment and ensuring sustainable development.

Finally, expanded broadband access is crucial in today's interconnected world. It enables individuals to access educational resources, work opportunities, and information that are essential for personal and economic growth. Expanding broadband access will bridge the digital divide, ensuring that no one is left behind in the increasingly digitalized world.

In conclusion, the revival of America's infrastructure is a pressing need that requires significant investment and commitment. The state of the nation's infrastructure has reached a critical point, and it is essential that action is taken to address these issues. The proposed infrastructure plan presents an opportunity to not only improve the physical backbone of the nation but also create jobs, stimulate economic growth, and enhance the overall quality of life for Americans. It is crucial that the government and stakeholders come together to prioritize infrastructure revival and rebuilding for the benefit of current and future generations.

10. Opioid Epidemic: Healing Communities, Saving Lives

The opioid epidemic in America has become a significant public health crisis, affecting individuals, families, and communities across the country. The widespread use and abuse of opioids, including prescription painkillers and heroin, has led to a staggering number of overdose deaths and has put a strain on healthcare systems and law enforcement agencies. In order to address this epidemic and save lives, it is essential to focus on healing communities and implementing comprehensive strategies to combat opioid misuse.

One of the key elements in healing communities and saving lives in the face of the opioid epidemic is increasing access to treatment and recovery resources. This includes expanding the availability of medication-assisted treatment

(MAT), which combines medications, such as methadone or buprenorphine, with counseling and behavioral therapies to treat opioid use disorder. By making these treatments more accessible, individuals struggling with addiction can receive the support and care they need to overcome their dependence on opioids.

Additionally, efforts to destigmatize addiction and promote a greater understanding of substance use disorders are crucial in healing communities. Education and awareness campaigns can help reduce the shame and isolation that often accompany addiction, encouraging individuals to seek help and engage in treatment. By creating a supportive and empathetic environment, communities can better support those in recovery and prevent future substance abuse.

Furthermore, addressing the root causes of opioid misuse, including chronic pain and mental health challenges, is essential for saving lives and promoting overall well-being. This involves improving access to alternative pain management options, such as physical therapy, acupuncture, and non-opioid medications, as well as increasing the availability of mental health services. By addressing these underlying factors, individuals may be less likely to turn to opioids as a means of coping with pain or emotional distress.

In order to achieve lasting change and combat the opioid epidemic, collaboration between government agencies, healthcare providers, community organizations, and law enforcement is imperative. This includes implementing policies and initiatives aimed at reducing the overprescription of opioids, preventing diversion and illicit sales of prescription medications, and increasing access to naloxone, a life-saving medication that can reverse the effects of an opioid overdose.

The opioid epidemic has ravaged communities across the United States, leading to an unprecedented number of overdose deaths and impacting countless individuals and families. In order to effectively address this crisis, communities must come together to implement comprehensive strategies that encompass prevention, treatment, and support. By working collaboratively, communities can make a significant impact in combating the opioid epidemic and ultimately saving lives.

Prevention is key in addressing the opioid epidemic. Communities can take proactive measures to educate individuals about the dangers of opioid misuse and provide resources for early intervention. This can be accomplished through community outreach programs, educational initiatives in schools, and partnerships with healthcare providers to promote responsible opioid prescribing practices. By raising awareness and providing information about the risks associated with opioid use, communities can empower individuals to make informed decisions and prevent opioid misuse before it begins.

In addition to prevention efforts, communities must also prioritize access to comprehensive treatment for those struggling with opioid addiction. This includes expanding access to evidence-based treatments such as medication-assisted therapy, counseling, and behavioral therapy. By investing in treatment resources, communities can ensure that individuals have the support they need to overcome addiction and begin the journey toward recovery. This also involves addressing the stigma associated with opioid addiction and providing non-judgmental support for those seeking help. By creating a supportive and welcoming environment, communities can encourage individuals to seek treatment and embark on a path toward healing.

Moreover, communities can play a crucial role in providing ongoing support for individuals in recovery from opioid addiction. This includes offering resources for housing, employment, and social support to help individuals rebuild their lives after addiction. Peer support programs and community-based recovery groups can also provide valuable connections and encouragement for those in recovery. By fostering a sense of community and connection, communities can help individuals navigate the challenges of recovery and build a strong foundation for a healthier future.

By working together to implement these comprehensive strategies, communities can effectively address the opioid epidemic and save lives. Healing and recovery from opioid addiction is a long and challenging process, but with a multifaceted approach that addresses prevention, treatment, and support, individuals and communities can overcome this crisis and move toward a healthier future. Through compassion, resources, and determination, communities can make a meaningful impact in the lives of those affected by opioid misuse and create a pathway to healing and hope.

11. Cybersecurity: Safeguarding the Digital Frontier

Cybersecurity in America: Safeguarding the Digital Frontier

In the digital age, the importance of cybersecurity cannot be overstated. As technology continues to advance and our reliance on digital systems grows, the need to safeguard our digital frontier becomes increasingly critical. From personal data to national security, the implications of a cyber attack can be devastating. Thus, the United States must prioritize cybersecurity efforts to protect its citizens, institutions, and infrastructure from potential threats.

The digital frontier is constantly evolving, and with it, the tactics used by cybercriminals. Cyber attacks can take many forms, from ransomware and phishing scams to infrastructure attacks and espionage. These threats can target individuals, businesses, or even entire nations. Therefore, it is essential for the United States to invest in robust cybersecurity measures to defend against these diverse and ever-changing threats.

At the individual level, cybersecurity is crucial for protecting personal data and privacy. With the widespread use of digital devices and online services, individuals are at risk of becoming victims of cybercrime. Cybersecurity measures such as using strong, unique passwords, enabling two-factor authentication, and keeping software up to date are essential for safeguarding personal information. Additionally, education and awareness campaigns can help individuals recognize and avoid potential online threats.

On a larger scale, cybersecurity efforts must also extend to businesses and government institutions. The protection of sensitive corporate information, intellectual property, and critical infrastructure is vital to maintaining economic stability and national security. A cyber attack on a major corporation or government agency can have far-reaching implications, impacting not only the targeted entity but also its customers, partners, and the overall economy. Therefore, organizations must prioritize cybersecurity by implementing strong firewall systems, regular security audits, and employee training programs to mitigate the risk of cyber attacks.

In addition to securing the digital infrastructure, the United States must also focus on establishing international partnerships and agreements to combat cyber threats. Cyber attacks are often transnational in nature, making it crucial for nations to collaborate and share information to effectively address these threats. By working with allies and international organizations, the U.S. can strengthen its cybersecurity defenses and create a united front against cybercrime.

Cybersecurity is an increasingly critical aspect of our society, as we become more reliant on digital technology. It is essential to protect our digital assets and infrastructure from cyber threats. This entails enhancing cybersecurity measures at the individual, organizational, and governmental levels and investing in research and development. Additionally, fostering international partnerships and prioritizing cybersecurity efforts are crucial steps in mitigating the risks posed by cyber threats.

The government plays a significant role in setting and enforcing cybersecurity standards and regulations. Legislation focused on data protection, privacy, and breach notification can help create a more secure digital environment. Government agencies can also work with private sector organizations to exchange information and collaborate on cybersecurity strategies.

Moreover, continued investment in cybersecurity research and development can lead to the creation of innovative technologies and strategies to defend against emerging cyber threats. This investment can result in the development of cutting-edge tools and practices to enhance our cyber defenses and respond effectively to cyber incidents.

Collaboration and information-sharing between governments, private industry, and international partners are also crucial for combating cyber threats. By fostering these relationships, we can benefit from diverse perspectives and resources to strengthen our cybersecurity posture.

The importance of cybersecurity in safeguarding the digital frontier in America cannot be overstated. With our increasing reliance on digital technology, protecting our digital assets and infrastructure from cyber threats has become more crucial than ever. Enhancing cybersecurity measures at individual, organizational, and governmental levels is essential for ensuring a secure and resilient digital environment.

At the individual level, it is important for people to practice good cyber hygiene, such as using strong passwords, keeping software up to date, and being cautious when clicking on links or downloading attachments. Organizations also must prioritize cybersecurity by implementing robust security policies and protocols, conducting regular risk assessments, and educating employees about cyber threats and best practices for mitigating them. At the governmental level, laws and regulations should be continually updated to address the evolving nature of cyber threats, and investments should be made in research and development to stay ahead of cyber adversaries.

By prioritizing cybersecurity efforts, investing in research and development, and fostering international partnerships, the United States can mitigate the risks posed by cyber threats and uphold the integrity of the digital frontier. International cooperation is particularly important, as cyber threats do not respect borders, and collaboration with other countries can help in sharing threat intelligence and coordinating responses to cyber incidents.

Furthermore, cybersecurity is essential for protecting critical infrastructure, such as power grids, transportation systems, and financial networks, from cyberattacks that could have severe consequences for national security and public safety. Additionally, with the increasing prevalence of IoT (Internet of Things) devices, securing these interconnected devices is becoming increasingly important to prevent them from being exploited by cybercriminals.

In conclusion, cybersecurity is paramount in safeguarding the digital frontier in America. It requires a multi-faceted approach, involving efforts at the individual, organizational, and governmental levels, as well as collaboration with international partners. By taking proactive measures to enhance cybersecurity, the U.S. can reduce the risks posed by cyber threats and create a safer and more secure digital environment for all.

12. Criminal Justice Reform: From Punishment to Rehabilitation

Criminal justice reform is a topic that has gained increasing attention in America in recent years. The traditional approach to criminal justice has been focused on punishment, with a strong emphasis on incarceration as a means of holding offenders accountable for their actions. However, this approach has come under scrutiny for its failure to effectively reduce recidivism rates and for its disproportionate impact on minority and low-income communities. As a result, there has been a growing movement towards a more rehabilitative approach to criminal justice.

The shift from punishment to rehabilitation in the criminal justice system is a complex and multifaceted process. It involves rethinking the way that offenders are treated within the justice system, with a focus on addressing the underlying causes of criminal behavior and providing support and resources to help offenders reintegrate into society.

One of the key components of criminal justice reform is the reevaluation of sentencing laws and practices. Mandatory minimum sentences and three-strikes laws have led to a dramatic increase in the prison population, with many offenders serving long sentences for non-violent offenses. These policies have not only contributed to overcrowded prisons and strained resources, but have also had a devastating impact on individuals and families.

Additionally, the over-reliance on incarceration as a form of punishment has limited the availability of alternative sentencing options, such as drug courts, mental health courts, and restorative justice programs. These alternative approaches focus on addressing the root causes of criminal behavior and providing offenders with the support and resources they need to break the cycle of crime.

Another important aspect of criminal justice reform is the expansion of reentry programs and support services for individuals who have been released from prison. Many offenders face significant barriers to reintegration, including limited access to employment, housing, and education. This can lead to high rates of recidivism, as individuals struggle to find their footing in society after serving their sentence.

By focusing on rehabilitation, the criminal justice system can work to address these barriers and provide opportunities for individuals to successfully transition back into their communities. This can include providing job training and placement services, mental health and addiction treatment, and support for obtaining stable housing.

In addition to rethinking sentencing and reentry, criminal justice reform also involves addressing the systemic issues that contribute to the cycle of crime and incarceration. This includes addressing racial and socioeconomic disparities within the justice system, as well as investing in community-based programs and resources that can help prevent individuals from becoming involved in criminal activity in the first place.

The shift from punishment to rehabilitation in the criminal justice system signifies a monumental change in how individuals who have committed crimes are perceived and treated. Instead of simply punishing offenders for their actions, there is now a focus on addressing the root causes of criminal behavior and providing individuals with the resources they need to turn their lives around. This shift represents a fundamental reimagining of the way our society approaches crime and punishment.

By prioritizing rehabilitation over punishment, the criminal justice system acknowledges that individuals who have committed crimes are often struggling with complex issues such as addiction, mental illness, and poverty. Rather than simply locking them away and forgetting about them, rehabilitation seeks to understand and address these root causes in order to prevent future criminal behavior. This approach recognizes that many individuals who end up in the criminal justice system have not had access to the support and resources they need to thrive, leading them to make poor choices. By providing individuals with the tools they need to succeed, we can work to break the cycle of crime and incarceration, ultimately creating safer and more just communities for all.

Additionally, the shift from punishment to rehabilitation reflects a deeper understanding of human behavior and the factors that contribute to criminality. Instead of viewing individuals who have committed crimes as irredeemable, rehabilitation operates under the belief that everyone has the capacity for change and growth. By offering support and rehabilitation services, we can help individuals reintegrate into society and become productive members of their communities. This not only benefits the individual, but also has the potential to reduce recidivism rates and make our communities safer.

Furthermore, the emphasis on rehabilitation can lead to cost savings for society as a whole. Incarceration is an expensive endeavor, and by focusing on rehabilitation, we can redirect resources towards prevention and support services that can help individuals avoid entering the criminal justice system in the first place. By addressing the underlying causes of criminal behavior and providing individuals with the necessary support, we can ultimately reduce the burden on the criminal justice system and lead to more positive outcomes for everyone involved.

In conclusion, the shift from punishment to rehabilitation in the criminal justice system represents a significant departure from traditional approaches to crime and punishment. By prioritizing rehabilitation, we can work to address the root causes of criminal behavior, provide individuals with the support they need to succeed, and ultimately create safer and more just communities for all. This approach reflects a deeper understanding of human behavior and has the potential to break the cycle of crime and incarceration, leading to better outcomes for individuals and society as a whole.

13. Affordable Housing: Sheltering Dreams For All

Affordable housing is a fundamental human right, yet in America, it remains a dream out of reach for many individuals and families. The lack of affordable housing has far-reaching implications, impacting not only individuals' ability to find shelter, but also their overall well-being, economic stability, and access to opportunities. In a country as wealthy and advanced as the United States, the need for affordable housing is a critical issue that demands attention and action.

One of the main challenges facing affordable housing in America is the lack of available options for low-income individuals and families. With housing costs continually rising, many people find themselves struggling to afford a place to live. This leads to a cycle of instability, as those who cannot find affordable housing may be forced to live in unsafe or inadequate conditions, or to prioritize housing costs over other essential needs such as food and healthcare.

Furthermore, the lack of affordable housing perpetuates inequality and limits opportunities for upward mobility. Without stable and affordable housing, individuals and families are unable to establish roots in a community, access quality education, or adequately plan for their future. This can have a long-term impact on individuals' ability to build a better life for themselves and their families.

In addition to the personal impact, the lack of affordable housing also puts a strain on local communities and the economy as a whole. Homelessness and housing instability can lead to increased strain on public resources, healthcare systems, and social services. It can also impact productivity as workers struggle to find stable housing, leading to absenteeism and decreased job performance.

Addressing the issue of affordable housing in America is not a simple task, but it is an essential one. It requires a comprehensive approach that includes policy changes, increased funding for affordable housing programs, and the development of affordable housing units. It also requires a shift in mindset and a recognition of affordable housing as a basic human right.

Affordable housing is a pressing issue that affects countless individuals and families across the United States. While there are examples of successful affordable housing initiatives, it is evident that more needs to be done to ensure that everyone has access to safe, stable, and affordable housing.

One example of a successful affordable housing initiative is the Low-Income Housing Tax Credit (LIHTC) program. This federal program provides tax incentives to developers to build affordable rental housing for low-income individuals and families. The LIHTC program has helped to finance over 2.8 million affordable rental units since its inception in 1986, providing much-needed housing for those in need.

Another successful example of affordable housing is rent control measures implemented in cities such as New York and San Francisco. Rent control helps to stabilize housing costs for tenants, allowing individuals and families to remain in their homes without fear of drastic rent increases. These measures have been instrumental in protecting vulnerable populations from displacement due to skyrocketing housing costs.

Despite these successes, the demand for affordable housing still far outweighs the available supply. According to the National Low Income Housing Coalition, there is a shortage of 7 million affordable and available rental homes for extremely low-income renters. This shortage creates a significant barrier for individuals and families struggling to make ends meet, forcing many to live in substandard or overcrowded housing, or to experience homelessness.

In addition to the shortage of affordable housing, many individuals and families face discrimination and barriers to accessing housing due to factors such as race, ethnicity, disability, and criminal history. These systemic issues further perpetuate housing inequality and contribute to the cycle of poverty and homelessness.

It is clear that addressing the lack of affordable housing in America requires a multifaceted approach. This includes implementing policies that incentivize the construction of affordable housing, expanding rent control measures, and addressing systemic inequalities in the housing market. It also requires a shift in societal attitudes towards affordable housing, recognizing it as a fundamental human right rather than a privilege.

Affordable housing is not just a social issue but also an economic one. Stable housing is a crucial foundation for individuals and families to thrive, allowing them to access education, employment, and healthcare. Additionally, affordable housing initiatives stimulate economic growth by creating jobs in construction and related industries and generating revenue for local governments.

In conclusion, affordable housing is a critical issue that affects individuals, families, communities, and the economy as a whole. It is a fundamental human right and should be treated as such. Addressing the lack of affordable housing in America is a complex but necessary task that requires both policy changes and a shift in societal attitudes. By recognizing the importance of affordable housing and taking action to address the issue, we can work towards sheltering the dreams of all individuals and ensuring that everyone has the opportunity to build a better future for themselves and their families.

14. Student Loan Crisis: Empowering the Future Generation

America's student loan crisis has reached a critical point, with an estimated 45 million borrowers collectively owing nearly $1.7 trillion in student loan debt. This crisis not only affects the current generation of young adults, but it also has far-reaching implications for the future of our nation. As the burden of student loan debt continues to grow, it is imperative that we take action to empower the future generation and ensure that they have the means to succeed.

One of the most pressing issues in the student loan crisis is the impact it has on the financial well-being of young adults. Many recent graduates find themselves struggling to make ends meet as they are burdened with monthly loan payments that significantly impact their ability to save, invest, and build wealth. This financial strain can also hinder their ability to take risks, pursue entrepreneurial ventures, or invest in further education, ultimately limiting their future potential.

Furthermore, the student loan crisis also has broader economic implications. As more and more young adults are saddled with significant debt, they are less likely to be able to afford to purchase homes, start families, or contribute to the economy in meaningful ways. This can have a ripple effect, impacting economic growth and productivity in the long term.

In order to address the student loan crisis and empower the future generation, it is imperative that we take a multipronged approach. First and foremost, we must work to make higher education more affordable and accessible. This includes increasing funding for public universities and community colleges, as well as expanding scholarship and grant programs for low-income students. Additionally, we must work to address the rising cost of tuition and fees, which have far outpaced inflation in recent years.

In addition to making education more affordable, it is crucial to address the student loan crisis in America by implementing reforms to the student loan system. The burden of student loan debt has become a significant obstacle for many young adults, inhibiting their ability to achieve their full potential. Therefore, it is imperative to explore options for loan forgiveness and debt relief, especially for borrowers who are struggling to make payments.

One of the key reforms that must be considered is implementing loan forgiveness programs for individuals who are facing financial hardship. This could involve forgiving a portion of the outstanding loan balance for borrowers who have been making consistent payments over a certain period of time. Additionally, there should be a focus on providing debt relief for borrowers who are experiencing extreme financial difficulties, whether due to unemployment, disability, or other challenging circumstances.

Furthermore, there is a pressing need to enhance transparency and education around student loans. Many young adults may not fully understand the implications of taking out student loans, and may not be aware of the options available to them for repayment or forgiveness. By providing more comprehensive education and resources, individuals can make informed decisions about their education and borrowing, ensuring that they are equipped with the knowledge necessary to manage their finances responsibly.

In addition to loan reforms and education, it is essential to empower the future generation with resources and support for career advancement and financial literacy. This includes expanding job training and apprenticeship programs, which can provide opportunities for individuals to gain valuable skills and experience in their chosen field without accumulating substantial debt.

Moreover, financial literacy programs can help young adults develop the necessary skills to manage their finances effectively and plan for their future.

In conclusion, the student loan crisis in America is a pressing issue that demands immediate attention. By working to make education more affordable, reform the student loan system, and provide support for career advancement and financial literacy, we can empower the future generation and ensure that they have the means to succeed. Ultimately, these efforts can contribute to a future where young adults are not burdened by the overwhelming weight of student loan debt, but instead are empowered to achieve their full potential.

15. Terrorism Threats: Securing a Safer Nation

Terrorism Threats in America: Securing a Safer Nation

The United States of America has long been a target of terrorism, with high-profile attacks such as 9/11, the Boston Marathon bombing, and the recent rise of domestic extremism. The ever-evolving nature of terrorism poses a constant threat to the security and safety of the nation. In response to these threats, the U.S. government has implemented various measures to mitigate the risk of terrorism and secure the country.

One of the most significant challenges in securing the nation from terrorism is the growing threat of domestic extremism. The rise of violent extremist ideologies, often driven by political, racial, or religious motives, has posed a serious threat to the safety and stability of the country.

The events of January 6th, 2021, demonstrated the real and immediate danger posed by domestic extremists and highlighted the urgent need for comprehensive and effective strategies to combat this threat.

Extremist groups and individuals are increasingly utilizing the internet and social media platforms to spread their ideology, recruit new members, and inspire attacks. The ability to radicalize individuals from a distance has made it more difficult for law enforcement and intelligence agencies to identify and disrupt potential threats. This shift in tactics requires a new approach to countering extremism, one that involves collaboration with tech companies, utilizing digital literacy programs, and enhancing efforts to monitor and counter online propaganda and recruitment.

In addition to domestic extremism, the United States faces a persistent threat from international terrorism. Transnational terrorist organizations such as Al-Qaeda, ISIS, and their affiliates continue to pose a significant threat to the security of the nation. These groups have demonstrated their ability to carry out sophisticated and coordinated attacks, making it imperative for the U.S. government to remain vigilant and proactive in countering these threats.

The United States has made significant progress in securing the nation from terrorism, however, the threat landscape continues to evolve, requiring ongoing adaptation and innovation in counterterrorism strategies. The growing influence of online radicalization and the proliferation of emerging technologies present new and emerging threats that the U.S. government must remain adaptive and agile in addressing.

To address these complex and multifaceted terrorism threats, the U.S. government has adopted a multi-pronged approach, involving law enforcement, intelligence agencies, and diplomatic efforts. In recent years, the government has increased its focus on prevention and intervention programs to identify and mitigate the risk of radicalization and violent extremism. The expansion of community-based initiatives, such as countering violent extremism (CVE) programs, aims to address the root causes of radicalization and extremism, fostering partnerships between law enforcement and local communities to prevent and respond to potential threats.

Another dynamic challenge is the proliferation of emerging technologies. From drones to artificial intelligence, terrorists are continuously adapting and leveraging new technologies to carry out attacks and evade detection. For example, drones have been used to deliver explosives, conduct surveillance, and disrupt critical infrastructure. To address this emerging threat, the U.S. government must invest in research and development of technological solutions, enhance cybersecurity measures, and collaborate with private sector partners to stay ahead of the curve.

To effectively address the evolving terrorism threat, the U.S. government must prioritize prevention, intervention, intelligence-sharing, and international cooperation. Prevention efforts should focus on addressing the root causes of radicalization, such as socio-economic disparities, grievances, and societal marginalization. Intervention programs, such as rehabilitation and de-radicalization initiatives, are essential in addressing individuals who have already been radicalized. Intelligence-sharing and coordination with foreign allies are crucial for identifying and disrupting transnational terrorist networks.

Furthermore, the U.S. governments should prioritized intelligence and information-sharing efforts to identify and disrupt potential terrorist plots. Enhanced coordination between federal, state, and local law enforcement agencies, as well as international partners, has been crucial in identifying and apprehending individuals involved in terrorism-related activities.

Additionally, the government has sought to address the financing of terrorism through initiatives to disrupt the flow of funds to terrorist organizations and networks.

Lastly, prioritization of international cooperation and engagement to counter the threat of terrorism is very important. The United States has forged strategic partnerships with other countries to disrupt terrorist networks, prevent the spread of violent extremism, and address the root causes of terrorism. Through diplomatic and multilateral efforts, the U.S. has worked to strengthen global counterterrorism capabilities and promote international cooperation in combating terrorism.

In conclusion, the United States faces a complex and evolving terrorism threat that requires comprehensive and multifaceted responses to ensure the security and safety of the nation.

However, the challenge of terrorism requires ongoing vigilance, adaptation, and innovation to stay ahead of the threat and safeguard the nation from harm. International cooperation and engagement in counterterrorism efforts are essential for addressing threats that originate beyond U.S. borders.

16. Substance Abuse: Breaking the Chains of Addiction

For decades, substance abuse has plagued America, tearing apart families, communities, and individuals. The chains of addiction have gripped countless individuals, leaving devastation in their wake. But there is hope on the horizon, as brave souls in every corner of the country are stepping up to break the chains of addiction and create a brighter future for all.

In the heart of the Midwest, a small town was once ravaged by the grip of opioids. Families watched in despair as their loved ones fell victim to the deadly allure of prescription painkillers and heroin. The town became a shadow of its former self, with crime rates soaring and hope dwindling.

But then, a group of determined individuals banded together to bring about change. They organized support groups, raised awareness, and provided resources for those struggling with addiction. They refused to let the chains of addiction tighten their grip on the community any longer.

In the bustling cities of the East Coast, a similar story was unfolding. Bright young minds were wasting away under the weight of alcohol and drugs. The streets were filled with broken spirits, desperately seeking solace in their next fix. But a group of dedicated professionals and volunteers refused to turn a blind eye to the suffering around them. They opened rehabilitation centers, offered counseling services, and fought for policies that would make it easier for those in need to access help.

Meanwhile, on the sun-drenched shores of the West Coast, a different battle was being fought. The allure of party culture and easy access to drugs and alcohol made it easy for many to fall into the clutches of addiction. But a growing movement of activists and advocates were determined to change the narrative. They organized outreach programs, created educational campaigns, and worked tirelessly to debunk the myths surrounding addiction and recovery.

In the midst of the opioid epidemic, America was caught in a relentless cycle of destruction and despair. Families were torn apart, individuals lost their way, and communities were left reeling from the devastation of substance abuse. But in time, the tides began to turn.

As awareness spread and resources were mobilized, communities once ravaged by addiction began to heal. Rehab centers opened their doors, providing support and treatment for those struggling with substance abuse. Families, who had been torn apart by the grip of addiction, sought reconciliation and found hope in the promise of recovery.

Individuals who had once been lost in the throes of addiction found purpose and direction. They enrolled in support groups, sought counseling, and embarked on the challenging but rewarding journey of recovery. With each step forward, the chains of addiction began to loosen their grip, and the darkness that had shrouded America began to lift.

Though the battle against addiction is far from over, the light of hope is shining through the darkness. The stigma surrounding substance abuse is being dismantled, and individuals are finding the courage to speak out and seek help. The government is investing in treatment and prevention programs, and communities are coming together to offer support and resources to those in need.

As America breaks free from the chains of addiction, a new chapter is unfolding. Families are reuniting, communities are rebuilding, and individuals are reclaiming their lives. The journey to recovery is filled with challenges and setbacks, but the momentum of change is undeniable.

In the face of adversity, America is rising. The tides have turned, and the promise of a brighter future is on the horizon. With determination and resilience, the nation is taking bold strides towards a healthier, more hopeful tomorrow. And though the road ahead may be long and arduous, the spirit of unity and perseverance is guiding America towards a future free from the grip of addiction.

17. Privacy in the Digital Age: Balancing Security and Freedom

Privacy in the digital age has become a precarious and complicated issue in America. With the rapid advancement of technology, the line between security and freedom has become increasingly blurred. The need for digital security and the protection of personal information has become a top priority for both individuals and the government. However, the measures taken to ensure this security often infringe on the right to privacy and freedom. It is crucial to strike a balance between the two in order to maintain a functional and just society.

On one hand, the digital age has brought about numerous benefits and conveniences. From the ability to connect with loved ones across the globe to the ease of access to vast amounts of information, the digital era has revolutionized the way we live. However, the overreaching power of technology has also led to a mass collection of personal data. From online shopping habits to social media activity, our digital footprints leave a trail of personal information that can easily be exploited if not protected.

In response to this, the government has implemented various surveillance programs and laws to monitor and collect digital data in the name of national security. The Patriot Act, for example, was passed in the wake of the 9/11 attacks and gave the government expansive powers to monitor and collect communications data in an effort to prevent future acts of terrorism. Similarly, the NSA's mass surveillance program, revealed by Edward Snowden in 2013, exposed the extent to which the government was monitoring and collecting digital information. While these measures were put in place to ensure the safety and security of the American people, they have raised serious concerns about privacy and civil liberties.

Tech companies have also come under fire for their handling of personal information. The Cambridge Analytica scandal in 2018 shed light on how social media platforms were collecting and selling user data without their knowledge or consent. This blatant invasion of privacy sparked a global conversation about the ethical and legal implications of data privacy in the digital age.

In the digital age, privacy is indeed a nuanced concept. On one hand, governments must secure their citizens against threats, necessitating levels of surveillance. On the other hand, individual privacy is a cornerstone of democratic freedoms.

A key aspect is transparency. Governments and corporations should clearly communicate their data practices. People should know what data is collected and how it's used. Clear policies that protect user data from misuse are crucial.

Individual responsibility also plays a pivotal role. Staying informed about digital rights and employing security measures (like strong passwords, encryption, and mindful sharing online) helps safeguard personal information.

Moreover, legislation needs to evolve with technology. Laws like the General Data Protection Regulation (GDPR) in the EU reflect an attempt to align legal frameworks with the realities of data exchange.

Equally important is the need for robust oversight mechanisms. Watchdogs and regulatory bodies should have the power and tools to enforce privacy rights and address infringements effectively.

While the need for digital security is undeniable, it is crucial to find a balance that respects individual privacy and freedom. The Fourth Amendment of the United States Constitution protects citizens from unlawful search and seizure, yet the digital age has created a gray area when it comes to what constitutes a "search" in the virtual realm. As technology continues to advance, the laws and policies surrounding digital privacy must evolve to keep up with the ever-changing landscape.

In order to achieve a balance between security and freedom in the digital age, it is important for lawmakers to enact clear and transparent regulations that protect individual privacy rights. This includes holding tech companies accountable for their handling of personal data and ensuring that government surveillance is conducted within the boundaries of the law. Additionally, individuals must take an active role in protecting their own privacy by being mindful of the information they share online and utilizing encryption and other security measures to safeguard their digital footprint.

By fostering a culture that values both security and privacy, and recognizing the responsibilities of all parties involved, we can move towards a society that respects individual rights while protecting collective security.

18. Gender Equality: Paving The Way For A Fairer Society

In the land of the free and the home of the brave, there has always been a struggle for equality. From the earliest days of the United States, gender inequality has been a dark stain on the fabric of our society. However, as we progress into the 21st century, there is a glimmer of hope on the horizon. With the rise of the feminist movement and the tireless efforts of activists, lawmakers, and everyday citizens, we are finally starting to pave the way for a fairer and more equitable society.

Gender equality in America has been a long and arduous battle. It wasn't until 1920 that women were granted the right to vote, and even then, the fight for equal rights and opportunities has been an uphill struggle. Women have been systematically excluded from many aspects of public and private life, including education, employment, and politics. The glass ceiling has been a persistent barrier for women in the workforce, and the gender pay gap continues to be a glaring injustice.

But the tides are turning. In recent years, there has been a groundswell of support for gender equality in America. The #MeToo movement has forced a reckoning with the widespread discrimination and harassment that women face in the workplace and beyond. High-profile cases of gender-based violence and discrimination have sparked a national conversation about the need for change. And with more women than ever before running for political office, there is a growing sense of possibility and hope for the future.

Paving the way for a fairer society means dismantling the systems of oppression and discrimination that have held women back for far too long. It means creating equal opportunities for all individuals, regardless of their gender. It means ensuring that all voices are heard and all perspectives are valued. Gender equality is not just a women's issue – it's a human rights issue, and it affects us all.

In order to achieve gender equality in America, it is crucial that we work together to address the root causes of inequality. This is not a task that can be accomplished overnight, but it is one that we must commit to wholeheartedly. It is imperative that we challenge the stereotypes and prejudices that perpetuate discrimination and bias. We must be vigilant in recognizing and addressing these harmful attitudes and working to dismantle them at every level of society.

It is also essential that we create policies and programs that promote equal access to education, employment, and healthcare. This means not only ensuring that these opportunities are available to all, but also actively working to eliminate the barriers that prevent individuals from accessing them. We must strive to create a society in which everyone has an equal chance to succeed, regardless of their gender.

Furthermore, it is crucial that we hold those in power accountable for their actions and decisions. This includes not only our elected officials, but also those in positions of influence in our communities, businesses, and organizations. We must demand fairness and equality in all aspects of our society, and we must hold those who perpetuate inequality to the highest standards.

The road to gender equality may be long and challenging, but the destination is worth the journey. A fairer society benefits everyone, and it is up to us to pave the way for a better future. By working together, we can build a more just and equitable America for all. Let us commit ourselves to this vital work, and let us strive to create a society in which everyone has an equal chance to thrive.

19. Aging Population: Embracing the Challenges of Tomorrow

As the population in America continues to age, the challenges and opportunities that come with an aging population are becoming more apparent. With a longer life expectancy and declining birth rates, the shape of American society is changing, and it is crucial for us to embrace the challenges of tomorrow.

The aging population in America is a result of a variety of factors. Advances in medicine and healthcare have led to longer life expectancies, while declining birth rates have contributed to an overall older population. This demographic shift has significant implications for various aspects of society, including healthcare, the economy, and social structures.

One of the most pressing challenges of an aging population is the increased demand for healthcare and long-term care services. As people live longer, they are more likely to require medical attention and support in their later years. The healthcare system will need to adapt to this shift, ensuring access to care for older individuals while also addressing the financial burden of increased healthcare costs. Additionally, the need for long-term care services, such as nursing homes and assisted living facilities, will also rise, posing a challenge for families and the healthcare system to provide adequate care for older individuals.

Economically, an aging population presents both challenges and opportunities. While older individuals may require more healthcare and long-term care services, they also bring valuable skills and knowledge to the workforce. Many older adults are choosing to continue working past traditional retirement age, contributing to the economy and filling labor shortages in various industries. At the same time, the strain on social security and pension systems will need to be addressed to ensure financial stability for older individuals.

Socially, an aging population necessitates a shift in how we approach community and support systems. With more older individuals living longer and often alone, there is a growing need for social support and connection. Communities will need to consider how to provide resources and social opportunities for older adults, addressing issues such as isolation and loneliness.

The aging of the population is a trend that is evident in many developed nations, including the United States. While it presents certain challenges, such as increased healthcare costs and a shrinking workforce, it also brings with it numerous opportunities for innovation and growth. As the population ages, there is a growing need for new technologies, services, and infrastructure to address the unique needs of older individuals.

One area in which innovation is particularly crucial is healthcare. As the number of older adults increases, there will be a greater demand for healthcare services and advancements that cater to the specific health challenges faced by this demographic. This could include the development of new medical treatments, the use of telemedicine to provide care to those in remote or underserved areas, and the creation of specialized care facilities for individuals with complex healthcare needs. By investing in healthcare innovation that caters to the needs of an aging population, we can ensure that older adults receive the high-quality care they deserve.

Furthermore, the aging population also presents opportunities for innovation in the design of age-friendly communities. This could involve creating more accessible public spaces, implementing transportation options that cater to older adults, and developing housing that is designed to accommodate the needs of older individuals. By embracing innovative designs that cater to the needs of older adults, we can create communities that allow individuals to age in place and remain active and engaged in their surroundings.

Another area ripe for innovation is the workforce. As the population ages, there will be a need to adapt the workforce to accommodate older individuals who may choose to continue working past traditional retirement age. This could involve creating flexible work arrangements, providing training opportunities to keep older workers up to date with new technologies, and fostering a work culture that values the experience and knowledge that older workers bring to the table.

In conclusion, while the aging of the population presents certain challenges, it also brings with it numerous opportunities for innovation and growth. By investing in healthcare advancements, age-friendly community design, and workforce adaptations, we can create a society that values and supports individuals of all ages. By acknowledging and addressing the challenges of an aging population, we can embrace the opportunities that come with it and build a brighter future for America.

20. Trade Policies: Navigating Global Partnerships

Trade policies in America have always been a contentious issue, and navigating global partnerships has become increasingly challenging in recent years. The United States has historically been a leader in international trade, and its policies have had a significant impact on the global economy. However, as the world becomes more globalized and interconnected, the need for effective trade policies that benefit both American businesses and consumers, as well as its global partners, has become increasingly important.

One of the key challenges in navigating global partnerships is the balance between promoting free trade and protecting domestic industries. While free trade can stimulate economic growth and increase the variety and quality of goods available to consumers, it can also lead to job losses and increased competition for domestic industries. As a result, trade policies must carefully navigate this balance, ensuring that American businesses remain competitive while also fostering positive relationships with global partners.

Another challenge in navigating global partnerships is the increasing complexity of international trade agreements and regulations. The rise of global supply chains and the interconnectedness of the global economy have made it more difficult to navigate the various rules and regulations that govern international trade. As a result, trade policies must be able to effectively navigate these complexities in order to ensure that American businesses can compete internationally and access global markets.

In recent years, the United States has faced significant challenges in navigating its trade policies and global partnerships. The Trump administration's "America First" approach to trade has led to increasing tensions with many of America's key trading partners, including China, Canada, and the European Union. These tensions have resulted in trade wars, retaliatory tariffs, and increasing uncertainty in the global economy.

In response to these challenges, the Biden administration has signaled a shift towards more cooperative and multilateral trade policies. President Biden has expressed a commitment to rejoining international agreements such as the Trans-Pacific Partnership and the Paris Climate Accord, as well as working with global partners to promote fair and free trade. This shift in approach has the potential to strengthen America's global partnerships and improve its position in the global economy.

Navigating global partnerships in trade requires a careful balance between promoting American interests and fostering positive relationships with global partners. As the world becomes more interconnected, the need for effective and cooperative trade policies has become increasingly important. By navigating these challenges successfully, the United States can strengthen its position in the global economy and promote economic growth and prosperity for both its businesses and its global partners.

One of the key factors in navigating global partnerships in trade is finding a balance between promoting American interests and fostering positive relationships with global partners. While it is important to prioritize American interests, it is also essential to recognize the interconnectedness of the global economy and the benefits of working collaboratively with international partners. This requires a nuanced approach that takes into account the diverse interests and needs of different countries while also advancing American economic goals.

In navigating global partnerships, it is important for the United States to prioritize fair and reciprocal trade agreements that benefit both

American businesses and global partners. This means negotiating agreements that open up new markets for American goods and services while also ensuring that global partners have equitable access to American markets. By promoting fair and reciprocal trade, the United States can strengthen its position in the global economy and create new opportunities for businesses to thrive both at home and abroad.

At the same time, the United States must also work to foster positive relationships with global partners in order to build trust and cooperation. This requires engaging in dialogue and cooperation with other countries to address common challenges and promote shared prosperity. By working collaboratively with global partners, the United States can build a network of allies and promote stability and economic growth both at home and abroad.

Navigating global partnerships in trade also requires a deep understanding of the complex web of economic, political, and cultural dynamics that shape international trade relations. This means carefully considering the impact of trade policies on different industries, workers, and regions, as well as the broader implications for global economic stability and security. By taking a comprehensive and strategic approach to trade policy, the United States can navigate global partnerships in a way that advances its economic interests while also promoting cooperation and stability in the global economy.

In conclusion, navigating global partnerships in trade requires a careful balance between promoting American interests and fostering positive relationships with global partners. By prioritizing fair and reciprocal trade agreements, fostering positive relationships with global partners, and taking a comprehensive and strategic approach to trade policy, the United States can strengthen its position in the global economy and promote economic growth and prosperity for both its businesses and its global partners. Through effective navigation of these challenges, the United States can build a more

prosperous and stable global economy that
benefits all stakeholders.

Note

This book is Written with meticulous research and a commitment to presenting diverse perspectives, "America Unmasked" offers valuable insights into the critical issues shaping the United States today. This book aims to ignite meaningful conversations, empower readers with knowledge, and inspire informed action towards a brighter future for all Americans.